A Tenement Childhood

A collection of poems by
Edith Little

White-washed ceilings
Waxcloth floors,
Shining brasses
Dark varnished doors
Kitchen range and recessed bed
This book recalls
The life we led.

Published by:
Richard Stenlake, Ochiltree Sawmill, The Lade
Ochiltree, Ayrshire, KA18 2NX. Tel: 01290 700266

Printed by:
Adlard Print & Typesetting Services,
The Old School, The Green,
Ruddington, Notts NG11 6HH

ISBN 872074 50 2

Some closes were wally,
While others were plain
A great place to play
If it started to rain,
Brass name plates on doors
Which the dampness made dim,
And finger marked handles
Considered a sin.

THE STAIRCASE WINDOW

"Grannie can I go oot an' play"
"I'll no' go very far"
"No, yer mither's awa tae a funeral
So jist bide whaur ye are!."

"Grannie please, can I play on the stair
I'll no' go oot in the rain
I jist want tae look at yon bonnie glass
On the staircase window pane."

"Oh here's the key ... awa ye go ...
Now dinna dirty yer dress
Dear only knows whit you get tae see
In yon bits o' coloured gless!"

I can look at a world of blue
Clouds, grass and flower bed
Then in an instant a fire like glow
As I squinted thru' the red.

A sunny world would soon appear
As I peeped up thru' the amber
Glinting gold on the wash-house roof
Our cat had tried to clamber.

I gazed once more thru' blue and red
Returning again to the amber
Yes, I thought, this sunlit world
Is the one I want to remember.

HOME MADE SOUP

Soup made with mutton flank
Or wee bit shank o' lamb
Sometimes thick wi' peas
Simmerin' alang wi' ham.

Lang afore ye turned yer fit
An' headed for the stair
You could smell ma mither's soup
As it wafted on the air.

While I ate it up ... her words
Around the table flew
Dark crusts will gey ye curls
An' soup stick tae yer ribs like glue!

Fish bones would supply the brains
Carrots mak me see
Oh, Mither a' the things you said
Hiv a' turned oot a lee.

I crack ma ribs gar I gey a cough
Wear thick specs an' carry a stick
My hair is straight, and like my brain
It's grey and short and thick!

Often when I make soup noo,
It comes frae oot a packet ...
I mind o' plates that filled me foo,
And man ... ye canna whack it!

AWFY BRAW

Awthing had to be braw, her doorstep white as
snaw
Everything sparkled inside as well
Curtains starched till they stood thersel',
Near broke her heart when the kettle steamed
And her kitchen window had just been
cleaned.

Spread her white things on the lawn
Checked the way the wind was blawin'
Scrubbed the claes pole, bleached the rope
Rinsed the sink, then wiped the soap.

Puir soul hersel' got taen awa
Lovely funeral, flooers an' a'
Fair prood wis she as she looked doon an' saw
Awthing wis BRAW ......AWFY BRAW.

THE WASH-HOUSE KEY

To they young ones here, who really don't know
How life was lived forty years ago
Houses were tenements with wally closes
Tiled to the top for the Toffee-Noses
We shared our sugar, we shared our tea,
Shared the squabbling, and the wash-house
    key.

Preparations went on the night before,
When the key came clattering through your
    door
The basket of clothes with the wringer on top
Wellies too, completed the props,
"Noo mind and leave oot yer dirty shirt,
And where's ma peeny to wrap roond ma
    skirt?"

The boiler fire didn't always light,
It could take three shots to get it right.
Orange boxes, and bits of old stick,
But a cup of paraffin did the trick.
On the day she washed we aye got MINCE,
I've never tasted the likes of it since…
She'd yell to the window, fair gon her dinger,
"Tell yer faither to put oot his ain dinner."

One had that key more than the rest,
Her man wore singlets, never vests,
"Been bilin' away from nine till four,
Think she'd never washed before,
Her on the landin' doon below,
Stuff hangin' oot just for show."

So, if your Grannie complains of her old
rheumatic,
Something stirs deep in her memory attic.
Pictures like these, when she climbed the stair,
Freezin cauld, and her back right sair,
Count yourself luckier than she's ever been,
When you flick on the switch of your washing
machine.

*One day per week was allocated to each
tenant in the close for the use of the wash-house,
then the key was passed on to the next. Much of
the stairhead conversation was, "Whose turn is
it for the key?" I can vividly remember two little
girls having a back green dispute which ended
by one of the pair tossing her head airily, and
saying with a sneer, "Your Mammy smokes in
the wash-house ...... mine doesn't."*

THE CLOOTIE DUMPLIN

At Christmas time an' birthdays,
Ma Maw aye went her mile,
An ott wid come the big pot
Wi watter on tae bile.
Ma Faither had to move his chair
Wi' moanin' an' wi' mumpin',
For Maw was gettin' ready
Tae mak her clootie dumplin'.

She got the flour an' treacle mixed,
In yon yella wally basin,
Ah get tae gey a wee bit steer
An try tae pinch a raisin.
"Where's the cloot tae pit it in?" –
She's at the shoutin' stage –
"Last time a ever saw it maw, wis roon the
    budgies cage."

"That's the kettle bilin', can you no move yer
    feet?"
Glowerin' at ma Faither dozin' in his seat.
"Dae ye have tae mak yer dumplin'
When am tryin' tae get a rest?
I'll awa an' get a pint" says he,
With sudden zest.
"Just you sit still an' listen,
An' don't gey me yer patter,
When that dries in, jist lift the lid
An' add mair bilin' watter."

"Noo keep that kettle bilin'
An' don't let the fire go oot,
Or there will be nae bloomin' dumplin'
Jist a lovely burned oot cloot."
I hoped we'd get some threepennies,
Wrapped up an' mixed as weel,
But she gets in an' awfu' state,
An' says it wilna sweel.

Ave watched the clock it's nearly time
Tae get the table ready,
Her dumplin' now is surely cooked
It's biled for three hours steady.

It's dryin' noo afore the fire,
Aw juicy plump an' tender,
Am scared in case the coal fa's oot
An' knocks it doon the fender
I'd love tae have a wee bit pick
But know I'd get a thumpin'
If I as much as took a look,
At ma Mammies clootie dumplin'.

THE AULD KIST

Gran aye kept them perfect, polished and
    clean
Wi' stuff you called elbow grease
There was no 'Mr. Sheen',
They were polished with love, the wood seemed
    to glow
There wasn't a corner that her duster didn't go.
An' we aye got a lecture that hers were the
    best
Some day they'd be mine alang wi' the rest...

An auld fashioned kist, a clumsy like thing,
I couldny help thinkin', they're gon in the bin
They were ugly an' heavy, but to her they were
    bonnie
And forever kept harpin' "They're solid
    mahogany."

The deep bottom draw is the one where she
    laid
Her blankets and linens, not one of them frayed
And tucked weel oot o' sight, but aye fine an'
    handy
Was Grannie's wee secret, "Napoleon Brandy".
Two drawers mair wi' roon wooden handles
Were stacked to the tap wi' nite-lites and
    candles
"I've sat in the dark for want o' a light
So I'm savin' them up in case o' a strike".

There's a wee secret drawer a' curved at the
front
Pulls out quite well, if you gey it a dunt
There's hairpins an' garters, bones from old stays
Even her teeth when she has her off-days,
Wee trinkets an' buttons, photos o' weans
Long since left their pram, but the memory
remains.

Now Grannie has gone and so have the
drawers
We've cleened oot the lot, save a few jeely
jaurs
I'm in a new hoose not a cupboard in sight
No space on my left, an' less on my right
Out come the suitcases frae under the bed
Back in go the claes from the season just shed.

A voice comes to me that sadly I've missed
Saying "What have you done wi' ma bonny
wee kist
Fine they'd have looked at the tap o' yer stair
I couldna stand suitcases o' ower ma flair..."
Oh yes I know now that Grannie was wise
As tiny tears prick the back of my eyes
I realise now and no doubt that you've
guesssed
That I wish I had kept the mahogany chest.

THE LINO

I've sailed the seven seas
Gone from East to West
Playing in the kitchen
Till telt tae "Hiv a rest".
Didn't need a passport
Or money for my fare
All I did was slide along
Ma mither's polished flair.

The best place was the lobby
From front door to the press
We skited roon her pot plant
Then sailed doon a' the rest
Put oor faither's socks on
Hand-knitted, thick and grey,
By the time we'd stopped oor slidin'
The sole was worn away.

The kitchen was our ocean
For sailing days to come
Sighted mony a harbour
In thon linoleum
The kitchen chairs turned upside doon
A dish cloth for a sail
We even had a ship's cat
And steered it by her tail.
Rowed through steamy jungles
Between bed recess and sink
Climbing on the bunker
Desperate for a drink.

Now I've sailed life's stormier seas
And come through quite a lot
But never likely to forget
The training that I got
Suffered many ups and downs
Blows I've felt richt sair
But nothing to the one you got
If Maw slipped on the flair ...

THE WEE BLACK BAG

Lying in the wardrobe drawer
With the book for paying the rent
Pulled out with all our valuables
Each time the siren went
The handbag she'd got for a birthday
Along with a bottle of scent ...

Time had worn the handles,
But the clasp was firm and good,
The leather unscratched and shiny,
With a frame like polished wood.
Inside lay all the papers
Marriage lines, certificates of birth,
Documents folded up neatly,
All going under the earth.
For whenever that siren sounded,
And to the shelter our feet we did drag,
A yell always came from the bed-room
"Haud on, till I get my wee bag"...

The guns had started to answer,
A warden was doing his nut,
"Come oan missus, a canny help it,
If the door o' yer wardrobe's got stuck,
An' yer son canny find his troosers,
Bide here, and yer chancin' yer luck."

That all-clear was finally sounded,
We knew it would be the last,
And they would have to start re-building
Homes flattened by bombing and blast,
Their contents had all been scattered,
Stubbed out, like the end of a fag,
I wonder now, did it all really happen,
And where is the wee black bag?

THE KITCHEN RANGE

It looked so grim and dirty when the fire was oot
The ashpan fu' o' cinders, or a guid fa' doon o' soot.
The kitchen looked so dreary wi' this monster at the
    wa',
The thocht o' hivin' to clean it wad mak you rin
    awa'.
The fire at once got kindled when you opened up
    the flue
Covered it wi' a newspaper, knelt in front and blew
A blaze at once got started, the coal now set alight,
With three big lumps on the fender for stoking up at
    night.

At one side sat the stewpan, an iron yin at that,
The other side, the ashet, rendering doon some fat.
The oven door a favourite place, for Tam, the family
    cat.
Rice pudding slowly baking, or jug of good beef tea,
The smell was aye that tempting, you had to look
    and see.

Maw hated all the cleaning, ZEBO, and emery cloth
She'd cover the floor with a newspaper
Then give vent to her wrath ...
My father had a brainwave, on nights that he
    worked late
The doors could go into his work, for thon Electro
    Plate,
Bits went in his pockets, ithers doon his pants,
While he was getting overtime, making guns for
    tanks.

By the time the war had ended, our fireplace looked
a treat,
Forever being inspected wi' neebours in the street,
Maw never had the cleaning, black-leading, an' the
like,
"Aw a dae is gey it a dicht, an' noo an' then a
wipe."
The intervening years have seen so many changes,
Now it appears, young couples are looking for auld
ranges.
I expect with unemployment, and many on the dole,
You really get your money's worth, out the one bag
of coal ...

Before modernisation and getting in an 'interior', it was the custom to have a kitchen range, which provided hot water, heating and cooking facilities. Sometimes it boasted of two gas rings on a metal frame which hooked up at the side by a brass chain when not in use.

My father worked in munitions, and the method of Electro Plating gave a lovely shiny chrome finish, which most people had done privately. My father worked a lot on nightshift and it appears it was much easier to get oven doors in and out when the bosses weren't around...

15

UNCLE DAVE

It was the same room and kitchen
He'd had since they were wed
We loved to go and see him
And his auld brass bed
Covered in white cotton
Tassels roon the foot
Taken to the washie at the first speck o' soot.

Short curtains at the windie
Lang lace yins at their side
How I loved to lift them
And pretend I was the bride
Gramophone in the corner
You could hear frae ben the room
I used to wind it up
Then waltz to a marching tune.

"See that picture on the wa'?"
He'd say, with admiration,
"Weel thon's yer Dad when he was a bairn,
I'ts ca'ed a third generation."
The kitchen table he never cleared
Jist used his ain big cup
Never bocht milk nor sugar
Just tinned stuff, we loved to sup ...
A Ghurka knife to cut the bread
"My army souvenir," he said.
And on the mantelpiece stood steel mortar
    shells
Whilst twa cheeny dugs had the fire tae thersels.

Contented he seemed to shuffle aboot
Aye wi' his baffies on the wrang foot
In his waistcoat pooch he'd fumble around
And a shiny sixpence always found.
I'll never forget that kindly old man
The tick of his clock, or the brass jeely pan
His "Come in an' sit doon, an' gey me yer
crack."
His face at the window each time you looked
back
Even today, although seldom I pass
I glance at the window, all shiny new glass
Hands clenched in my pockets, for fear I should
wave
For I'm certain I'm seeing Auld Uncle Dave ...

*Uncle Dave and Auntie Lebe were a devoted
couple until her death. He was my father's uncle,
at one time a regular soldier in the Black Watch,
and had served in India. He had us spellbound
with his stories, and particularly the one of how
he acquired the Ghurka knife.*

EASTER EGGS

It seems a lot of money
And you can't afford the price
But to a child an Easter egg
Is something rather nice
All done up in ribbon
Wrapped in silver, often gold
With chocolates nestling inside
Quite often, I've been told.

My Grannie used to buy them
Every Easter, so you see
I know how little children feel
When she says "Just bide a wee,
There's a surprise behind my curtain
But first eat up yer tea."

We had to go by bus, then ferry half the way
My Grannie lived in Dundee, across the River
      Tay,
The tarry ropes were tied up
The boat would give a bump
A man with cap and dungarees
Was always first to jump
The cassies on the slip-way were wet and pretty
      steep
My mother kept on saying "Noo dinna weet yer
      feet."

We had to hurry up as the ferry had been late
Auntie used her lunch hour to meet us at the
gate
Then came the cheery tram ride
With constant clanging bell
Sliding on red leather, swaying from side to side
as well

I began to get excited, only one more stop to
go
Clanging uphill all the way
But awful, awful slow,
I spied the paper shop with fish nets, paraffin
and sticks
Where you ran to get a mantle if the gas light
needed fixed.

Around that magic corner, my Grannie I would
see
Looking out her window, looking just for me
A sudden dash, and three stairs up
I had wings instead of legs
For hidden behind her curatin
Would be my Easter eggs...

*Every Easter we went to my Mother's home in
Dundee, a week-end referred to by Dundonians
as "the Fast". We got hard-boiled eggs to
paint, and later rolled them down some grassy
bank in Baxter Park.*

THE BARROWS

It's freezing and it's damp, but they'll be at their stall,
Wrapped up in mufflers to keep oot the cauld,
Vacuum flasks and cups, haundless and cracked,
Gloves wi' half fingers to heal up the hacks,
Ankle boots and men's socks, who can be choosers,
Wi' yon draught blawin' up the leg o' yer troosers?

Dresses and coats, bundles o' bras,
"Of course it's yer size, but if it's too sma',
Gey it away to yer daughter-in-law."
"But I haven't got one", says I all uppy,
"Well a' I can say is yer bluidy lucky."

Plastic dishes and brooches, crystal beads and
     pearls,
Reflected by the light of the hot-dog stalls,
"Anorak, lady, not one bit second hand,"
Calls out the Paki vendor from behind his stand,
"I have all sizes here, pattern or plain,
Good for Glasgow weather, plenty lovely rain."

China cups and wally plates "Drap it missus it willny
     break"
"Lovely velvet curtains … fully lined,
Canny even see they've been jined."
"Maybe so, but I think they're faded,"
"For God's sake hen, that's the latest … aw shaded."
"I think I'll check my window and make sure it's
     seven feet"
"Aw weel then hen, jist please yersel,
But they'll no be here next week."

Toffee aipples, macaroon, and candy floss
"I don't make a profit, I'm selling at a loss."
"Heavy woven bed mats, lovely oan yer bed
If you canny turn beneath it, pit it oan the flair
instead,
Come oan Missus, buy wan, use it for a rug,
If yer man disny like it, gey it tae yer dug."

Sauntering doon the Trongate to dear old Glasgow
Cross,
There's naebody quite like them, each one his ain
wee boss,
A few resemble peacocks, but maist are plain wee
sparrows,
God may have made the birds, but Glasgow made
the Barrows.

THE MILK PAN

You sit there by the sink
The pan I've burned black,
I've got it fu' o' watter
An' a guid haunfu' o' sat.
You've been there a week or mair,
But a canna bear the thought
Of goin' oot an' gettin' anither milk pot.

I got ye when I merried in a set o' three,
The ither yins were bigger
So milk pan ye had to be.
You've seen eggs biled an' scrambled,
Or jist watter for the tea.
You looked so new and unscratched
Of guid metal you were cast
A relic from the days
When stuff wis made tae last.

I'll hiv tae throw ye oot,
But hivny got the heart.
You've been there on my cooker,
Right from the very start.
Whatever made me try to clean you,
I'll never really know,
But I scraped a wee bit black
And your sides began to show.
Some stronger stuff was needed,
So I donned a rubber glove.

I scoured an' scraped an' polished,
Wi' all a housewife's love
Put you back beside the others,
Gleaming in a row
And thought to myself quite proudly
It only goes to show,
That things are never half as black
As they seem at first you know...

FORTY WINKS

Feet up on the fender, paper on the floor,
I'm gonna hae ma forty winks
So dinna bang the door!
Dishes steepin' in the sink,
Watter no' richt heated yet,
So I'll jist hae ma forty winks,
While it's gettin' het.

The dogs hae baith been fed, an' lyin' at my feet,
I got the paper read, noo I'll hae a sleep.
I've had a busy day – washed doon a' the stair,
Polished a' the brasses, an' thon wee lobby flair.
Listened to yon neebor, the wan that's fu' o' moans,
She's aye got a pain and her voice even groans.
If I'm ever kept too long
An' canna thole her girnin'
I get someone to call me in –
"Come on the mince is burning"…

Yes, I've had a busy day, my hours are all that full,
Makin' soup an' stovies, bairns comin' in from school.
Now I'm getting drowsy, the fire is burning low
So if you see me fall asleep – just before you go,
Close the door behind you,
Leave the dishes in the sink.
I'll see to all that later…
When I've had ma forty winks.

THE WIRELESS

Our set was called an "ECHO", sat on the chest of
    drawers,
The hub of conversation during our generation's
    wars,
Listened to that fatal message, which we already
    knew,
Then Winston Churchill's famous speech, and what
    we'd have to do.
Ration books were issued, confection coupons too,
Shortages of paper ... no "Izal" for the loo,
Windows sealed with black tape, bulbs painted dark
    as night,
Warnings of being fined, if you didn't "Put out that
    light."

At one p.m. and six o'clock, despite each others
    views,
We were told to hold our tongues, we're listening to
    the news
Daren't make a sound, cough, or even sneeze,
I can still feel that dish-cloth, wet across my knees.
Psychologists today would gas-masks portray,
To ascertain that children didn't wince,
I was held in a chair, protesting "It's not fair",
The memory has terrified me ever since.

We had eggs that were dried, liquid "Un-Yun", when
    we fried
That slice of sausage, or two ounces of mince,
Turnip, boiled and cooled, completely had me
    fooled,
Flavoured with the essence of banana,
We ate tomato jam, sandwiches with Spam
And cake they had the nerve to call Sultana.

Nine o'clock, and "This is London", the chimes of old Big Ben

Would echo round our kitchen as we settled down again,

Messages came over, not making any sense,

Intended for the underground, waiting in suspense,

"Aunt Matilda will be late today." "The twins arrived on time."

"The grapes have ripened early, prepare now for the wine."

I don't look back in anger, as a child I knew no grief,

My children often ask me, (but please keep it brief),

I forget the deprivations, shelters, bombs and queues,

But I have something precious, which they are bound to lose,

The constant crunch of chocolate, chewy toffee underneath,

I tell them that sweet rationing, is how I've kept my teeth,

I had no Trani either when I learned of war and death,

So I stand a better chance as well of never being deaf...

SATURDAY MATINEE

Decayed, and falling down
Marble steps which used to gleam
Chromium handles on the door,
A man with silver buttons
Paced up and down the floor,
He glanced out at our faces
Huddled in the cold,
"Oh mister, gonny let us in?"
The big ones yelled and bawled.
He checks his watch against the hour
Five minutes more to go,
Those eyes begin to glower,
He'll stand soon in a corner
Protected from our feet
As everyone goes pushing by
To get a good front seat.

Shouting and shoving, trips to the jon
Warnings to stop our carrying on.
The lights are dimmed, and silence reigns,
Our world and all its colours change,
Every shade in the rainbow's hue
Brilliant orange to a deepening blue.
Curtains of satin slide along,
Who's on first? Pop-Eye, or Anna-May-Wong?
Half way through we suffer the news
Not interested in adults, or their views,
Except the ship, just launched on the Clyde
Wi' a picture hoose, an' swimmin' pool inside...

On with the show, it's Mickey Mouse
Then Peter Lorre in the Haunted House,
Suspense with the serial nearing its end,
The Lone Ranger has only one bullet to spend.
We argue going up the road, and who's got
money for chips
And discuss the heroes we left behind,
Till we see them next week at the Flicks...

Saturday was the highlight of our week. You got your pocket money, and money for the pictures.

Our local was the "Ascot", very plush in its day, or we went to the "Boulevard", where the interior decor appeared Spanish to me, with rough-cast walls, and wrought iron balconies. Most of our old haunts have been pulled down or turned into Bingo halls.

SPRING CLEANING

Dreary winter passed us by –
Wet wellies on the floor,
Pulley full of drying clothes,
And endless-seeming chore...
Were nothing to the upset
When Spring came in the door.
Gazing round the ceiling
We could hear that dreaded phrase
"Spring cleaning starts tomorrow,
So it's porridge and auld claes..."

The clothes basket held treasures
Which adorned our mantelpiece,
The mirror on the wall above
Supported clouds of fleece.
Blue vases with the waving fronds
Of imitation grass,
A miniature of Robert Burns
With ploughshare made of brass.

The largest rugs were lifted
And carted down the back,
Two cane carpet beaters
With their resounding whack!
Not until the dust had cleared
Would the beating stop,
Or some adjacent neighbour called
"It's efter eight o'clock!"

Every drawer turned inside out,
Fresh with paper lined,
Curtains stripped from windows
Dusting paper blinds.
Mattress hauled from off the bed,
While she dusted all the springs,
But "Leave thon picture oan the wa'
There's a big crack where it hings…"

This went on for five whole days –
Very near a week,
Home-made soup and stovies
Were all we had to eat.
When everything was back in place,
She beamed with pride and boasted:
"Aw weel, ah feel much better noo!"
Then collapsed in bed exhausted.

DOON THE WATTER

We wereny away that summer,
The weather wisny great,
So took a wee place later on
Jist tae gie the weans a break.
We got a hoose in Millport,
(A wee place doon the Clyde),
Three double beds, a couch,
Wi' toilet – a' inside!
I got awthing ready,
An' checked the time o' trains –
There's gonny be nae rushin'.
'Cause I've got varicose veins.

We reached the Central Station
Wi' half an oor tae spare,
Settled for a good long wait
On a hard, cauld widden chair.
Ye know of course what kids are –
Drive ye roon the bend,
Once they've got their money,
A' they dae is spend…
There's something aboot a station,
Desolate an' murky,
Especially sittin' on yer ain
Wi' a wan-eyed dug
An' a frozen turkey…

Eventually we got seated,
Turkey on the rack,
Dug sprawled up beside me
He's away at the back.
For a man who likes his forty fags,
I thocht he must be jokin' –
Lifts his paper an' saunters doon
To the door that says *NO SMOKING.*
I'm sittin' quietly dreamin',
When a' I hear is "Maw...
There's watter drippin' on that man's suit,
Yer turkey's startin' tae thaw!"

It was awfy quiet when we arrived,
No' the usual steer,
Awthing wis deserted,
Nae luggage on the pier.
We looked mair like a circus
Somebody had lost –
Four weans, a dug an' a turkey
Startin' tae defrost.
We glanced up at each other
Too fed up tae speak –
Naebody had telt us,
But it was their winter week...

BACK-GREEN CONCERT

Did you ever dance in the back-green
In costumes of paper crepe,
Hoping it wouldn't fall apart,
Or worse still ... soaking wet?

Neighbours flung open windows,
Fat elbows cushioned the sills,
And they all joined in the chorus
Sung by five little girls.

They sang "The Fleet's In Port Again"
Followed by "Run, Rabbit, Run".
Not everybody knew the words,
But they all joined in the fun.

Someone gave up their coupons
To buy us chocolate bars,
And for one afternoon in the back-green
The five of us were stars.

THE LAST TRAM

When the last tram went, that wasn't all...
We lost our cobbled streets,
And the friendly glow from gas-lit lamps,
Cosy fires and starched white sheets.

Something went with the last old tram,
A warmth escaped from our lives,
Along with Miss Cranston's tea-rooms,
High teas, with forks and knives.

Something else clattered out of our lives
With that clanging, jangly bell.
Will it return? Just wait and see:
Time alone can tell.

AULD PARTICK

Shattered window panes
Staring at the past,
Wondering what these metal arms
Are doing at the sill.
Slates fall like confetti,
Dust rises from inside,
She gazes at familiar walls
She lived in as a bride.

Wallpaper flutters, loose and damp,
(I mind he picked it, thon wee scamp),
Moved his bed to hide the tear,
Ripped the lino getting there.
Now it hangs for all to see –
Not everyone's choice, but it suited me.
That gap where my fireplace used to be,
Friends sat round with cups of tea,
(That chimney aye wis bad fur soot –
Wan gust o' wind an' the fire wis oot).

Old voices echo down the hall,
As neighbours' names I now recall.
Another sound breaks up my dreams,
While crackling flames eat up the beams,
Much louder than a pulley squeaking,
Dirtier than a chimney reeking –
A bulldozer now with menacing roar
Rips apart my treasure store.

A few more days – and nothing will remain,
A puddle maybe, if there's been some rain
No traces of the past in the mud and dust and brick,
But nothing lasts forever...
Even Auld Partick.

CLYDE-SIDE

The paddles turn, the waters churn,
I have no Paw, or even Maw to take me now
On journeys from the Broomielaw.
No sandshoes gleaming white
From drying in the oven overnight,
"Noo mind yer Paw's new claes,"
Says Maw, held in by her new stays,
While Paw surveys the banks wi' pride
Recalling ships launced on the Clyde.

No hammering now, nor smell of iron dust,
Just lapping water, stanchions red with rust.
Silent ferries where workers used to pour
Down wooden steps from Govan's shore,
Checkit bunnets, an' wee piece pokes,
Laughing, whistling, telling jokes.
While deep in their hearts lay the craftsman's
pride,
Their skill acclaimed, aye far an' wide,
Recalling tales of how they built a dream,
And each generation raised a "Queen".

MEMORY LANE

Don't go back ... it's better to remember,
You never feel the winter chill
In August or September
The house that you were born in,
Or the garden where the peony roses used to
    grow.
Don't go back, it's better to remember,
Familiar fields furrowed deep in winter snow,
Gas-lit lamps in the High Street,
The moon with its halo
Miss Jolly's sweet shop, tinkling bell and all,
Soor plooms, acid drops and home made
    candy balls.
Saturday morning at the smiddy door
The smell of singeing hooves
As golden sparks rain on the cobbled floor.

Don't go back ... it's better to remember,
The church up on the brae
Where you sat so quiet in Sunday school
Unravelling your jersey sleeve away.
Summer picnics on a farmer's cart,
Tin mugs and bales of hay ...
Don't go back ... it's better to remember
It doesn't ever rain that way,
And all the days of childhood
Seem filled with only sun
Don't go back ... it's better to remember
And memories are so much fun...